Literary Lunch

Literary Lunch

VINTAGE

1 3 5 7 9 10 8 6 4 2

Vintage
20 Vauxhall Bridge Road,
London SW1V 2SA

Vintage is part of the Penguin Random House group of companies
whose addresses can be found at global.penguinrandomhouse.com.

Penguin
Random House
UK

First published by Vintage in 2015

www.vintage-books.co.uk

A CIP catalogue record for this book is
available from the British Library

ISBN 9781784702083

Printed and bound by Clays Ltd, St Ives Plc

MIX
Paper from
responsible sources
FSC
www.fsc.org   FSC® C018179

Penguin Random House is committed to a sustainable future
for our business, our readers and our planet. This book is made
from Forest Stewardship Council® certified paper.

Contents

MAIN COURSES

DESSERTS

CONDIMENTS

Food in Fiction

Food and drink are the writer's friend. Faced with the need to establish a character as economically as possible, the novelist has many options. They have clothes for them to wear and routines for them to follow. They can record their speech patterns and challenge their creations' moral fibre with decisions made well or badly. But these things take time, and risk breaking the rule that they should show the reader who their characters are, rather than *tell* them.

Send their inventions out for lunch, however, and by their character's menu choices – perhaps just by the way they hold their fork – the job is quickly done. Memories of eating and taste are accessed more quickly than almost any other, so our own remembered food experiences do so much of the writers' job for them. From the moment the Bible's author portrayed woman as a creature of instinctive lusts who simply couldn't resist the lure of an apple in the Garden of Eden, what and how we eat has been the novelist's shorthand.

And shorthand it all too often is. Food in fiction isn't designed to give you meal plans. Rare is the novel with exact measurements.

It's all about appetite and good taste and personal preference. As long as the writer has done the job well, the reader will experience the character through the meal. If it's done really well the poor reader can also be left hungry: they want to taste the risotto our hero made to distract and soothe the thug holding him hostage; they want to try those delicate pastries our girl just comforted herself with in a Viennese cafe as a love affair turned to ashes.

Here, then, is a book designed to soothe those frustrations: a set of recipes born from the texts in which the food was first mentioned. Most cookbooks offer lists of ingredients and things to do with them. You then use that information to create a dish to put at the heart of your own personal drama. This book works the other way round – it starts with the drama, and invites you to extract from it the dish that got the action moving.

In doing so it invites us to examine the role food plays in fiction, for it is many and various, and is rarely just about appetites. Sometimes the culinary subtext is thumpingly obvious. When C. S. Lewis has Edmund tempted by the White Witch's Turkish Delight in *The Lion, the Witch and the Wardrobe*, he is lunging at a Christian symbolism so unsubtle it's a wonder the authors of Genesis didn't try to sue Lewis for copyright infringement. When, in *Ulysses*, James Joyce details Leopold Bloom's taste for 'grilled mutton kidneys which gave his palate a fine tang of faintly scented urine' he has his man nailed as a chap of earthy tastes in just 14 words. (If only Joyce had restricted himself to those 14 words.)

For some writers food is simply a scene-setting tool. In *Human Traces*, Sebastian Faulks describes how, at a dinner party in a nineteenth-century Austrian schloss, 'apricot Ischl tarts' are served. For those interested, Ischl tarts are delicate shaped biscuits layered with jam or preserve which, in the Mittel-European style, utilise ground almonds, though Faulks tells us none of this because it would not serve his purpose. For the author it is less about the delicacy of the tart than the verisimilitude: his story is set in a grand house with a grand kitchen so of course they would serve the local delicacy, Ischl tarts. Merely by using the word, he establishes a sense of place with its own exotic grandeur.

Booker Prize winner Julian Barnes has made very public his interest in food and drink, which he pursues with an English intellectual's precision. In his non-fiction book about his adventures in cooking, *The Pedant In the Kitchen*, he extols the virtues of the precise recipe, 'Why should a word in a recipe be less important than a word in a novel? One can lead to physical indigestion, the other to mental.' In his short story 'Home to Hemingway', his characters are light-heartedly playful on the subject. For them, food and drink serves as a vehicle for an extended gag about different kinds of writers – poets do quick stir fries, novelists long braises requiring stamina and so on – and happily there is a hearty lamb stew for the banter to take place over.

Elsewhere in fiction the food itself is the vehicle for the comedy. When, in *Bridget Jones's Diary*, our heroine uses blue string to bind the ingredients in her soup and the dye leaches out, we both love and despair of her. In one acute narrative detail – of adulthood grasped for in the shape of a grown-up dinner party, and then sabotaged by infantile naivety – writer Helen Fielding has given us vital information. In Susan Hill's novel, *The Various Haunts of Men*, her protagonist's choice of a prawn cocktail marks Simon Serailler out as a man who refuses to be cowed by the demands of fickle culinary fashion. Likewise when the dowager in Haruki Murakami's *IQ84* (Book 1) serves a *salade niçoise* we are to infer that she is a woman of simple pared back tastes.

And then there is Henry Perowne's seafood stew from Ian McEwan's novel *Saturday*. McEwan is renowned for his detailed research; he went as far as to observe neurological operations so he could accurately describe Perowne's work as a brain surgeon. But it is in the precision with which Perowne approaches the making of the fish stew that we finally understand the man. We are told he likes the fact that, 'In the kitchen the consequences of failure are mild... No one actually dies.' And yet Perowne still attends to the culinary details as if they might, as does the prose. This is one dish you could almost cook straight off the page of the novel. Every ingredient is there, every stage detailed.

Still, it's always good to have a few measurements. Happily, now you do.

STARTERS

Bridget's Blue Soup

from *Bridget Jones's Diary* by Helen Fielding

Friday 3 November

This will be the menu:

Velouté of Celery (v. simple and cheap when have made stock).

Char-grilled Tuna on Velouté of Cherry Tomatoes Coulis with Confit of Garlic and Fondant Potatoes.

Confit of Oranges. Grand Marnier Crème Anglaise.

Will be marvellous. Will become known as brilliant but apparently effortless cook.

Monday 20 November

8pm Ugh, do not feel like cooking. Especially dealing with grotesque bag of chicken carcasses: completely disgusting.

10pm Have got chicken carcasses in pan now. Trouble is, Marco says am supposed to tie flavour-enhancing leek and celery together with string but only string have got is blue. Oh well, expect it will be OK.

Tuesday 21 November

8.35pm Oh my god. Just took lid off casserole to remove carcasses. Soup is bright blue.

9pm Love the lovely friends. Were more than sporting about the blue soup, Mark Darcy and Tom even making lengthy argument for less colour prejudice in the world of food. Why, after all, as Mark said – just because one cannot readily think of a blue vegetable – should one object to blue soup? Fish fingers, after all, are not naturally orange.

RECIPE:

Serves 6

COOK'S NOTE:

For Bridget Jones's authentic 'blue soup', tie the leek greens
and celery with blue string before making the stock.

FOR THE STOCK

The green ends cut from 2 leeks (see below)

1 celery stick

1 chicken carcass

6 black peppercorns

1 bay leaf

FOR THE SOUP

1 tablespoon olive oil

1 shallot, finely chopped

2 leeks, white parts only, finely chopped
4 celery sticks, finely chopped
15g butter
1 large potato, around 350g, peeled and chopped
1 litre chicken stock
50ml double cream
Salt and freshly ground black pepper

First make the stock. Tie the green ends of the leeks together with the celery stick and put in a large pan. Add the chicken carcass, peppercorns and bay leaf and cover with 1.25 litres of cold water. Put a lid on the pan and bring gently to the boil. Half tilt the lid off the pan to allow some steam to escape, then simmer for 30 minutes.

Strain the stock into a jug; you should have 1 litre. If there's more, pour it back into the empty pan and simmer to reduce. If it's less, top up with cold water.

Heat the oil in a pan with 2 tablespoons of water and sauté the chopped shallot, leeks and celery over a low heat for 5–10 minutes, until the vegetables are soft, but not coloured. Stir in the butter and chopped potato and continue to cook for a further 5 minutes.

Pour in the stock, cover with a lid and cook for 10–15 minutes until the potatoes are completely tender.

Use a stick blender to whizz the soup until smooth. Add the double cream and bring gently to a simmer to reheat. Season to taste, then spoon into six bowls and serve.

Giovanni's Authentic Prawn Cocktail

from *The Various Haunts of Men*,
a Simon Serrailler novel by Susan Hill

The restaurant was a glowing warm oasis, one of the small, old-fashioned Italian places that made no concessions to interior design and twenty-first-century food fashion.

'I love it because it's straight out of the sixties,' Simon said, as they were greeted effusively by the proprietor and given a cosy table in an alcove near the window. 'Look, the candles really do come in Chianti bottles with straw waistcoats.'

The menus arrived, the specials of the day were described lovingly by a waiter with the sort of Italian accent people used to joke about. 'The difference is that the food is fantastic. There may be prawn cocktail but it contains huge, salty fresh prawns in the most wonderful creamy home-made mayonnaise and the veal is thin as tissue paper and the liver melts in your mouth.'

'The best sort of comfort food.'

A bottle of Chianti arrived and was poured, ruby red, into huge glasses.

'Comfort drink,' Simon lifted his to her and smiled, that devastating, extraordinary smile. The restaurant was full but there was no one else at all in the room, in Lafferton, in the world. This is happiness, Freya said, this, now. Perhaps I have never known what it was until tonight.

RECIPE:

Serves 4

2 egg yolks
150ml light vegetable oil, such as olive
1 tablespoon tomato chutney (ketchup can also be used here)
Splash of Worcestershire sauce
Splash of Tabasco
Juice of ¼ lemon, plus 2 slices, to serve
½ iceberg lettuce
400g large cooked and peeled prawns,
plus 4 shell-on prawns to garnish
Cayenne pepper, for sprinkling
Salt and ground white pepper

Put the egg yolks in a large bowl and whisk together. Whisk in a teaspoon of the olive oil until completely incorporated.

Continue to add the oil, a dribble at a time, whisking well between each addition. Slowly the mixture will turn from a smooth sauce to a thick mayonnaise. Once all the oil has been added, season well with salt and white pepper. Whisk in the tomato chutney, Worcestershire sauce, Tabasco and lemon juice. Taste and adjust the seasoning.

Finely shred the lettuce and divide among four bowls. Toss the prawns in a couple of tablespoons of the mayonnaise, enough to coat the prawns generously, then spoon evenly on top of the lettuce. Any leftover mayonnaise can be stored in an airtight container in the fridge for up to three days.

Cut each lemon slice in half, then put a little nick on the flat edge of each and position on the edge of the bowl, along with a whole prawn. Sprinkle over the cayenne pepper and serve.

Ezra's Heartening
Chicken Gizzard Soup

from *Dinner at the Homesick Restaurant* by Anne Tyler

He knew that after he left, someone would discard his soup. But this was his special gizzard soup that she had always loved. There were twenty cloves of garlic in it. Mrs. Scarlatti used to claim it settled her stomach, soothed her nerves – changed her whole perception of the day, she said. (However, it wasn't on the restaurant's menu because it was a bit 'hearty' – her word – and Scarlatti's Restaurant was very fine and formal. This hurt Ezra's feelings a little.) When she was well enough to be home, he had often brewed single portions in the restaurant kitchen and carried them upstairs to her apartment. Even in the hospital, those first few times, she could manage a small-sized bowl of it. But now she was beyond that. He only brought the soup out of helplessness, he would have preferred to kneel by her bed and rest his head on her sheets, to take her hands in his and tell her, 'Mrs. Scarlatti, come back.' But she was such a no-nonsense woman; she would have looked shocked. All he could do was offer this soup.

RECIPE:

COOK'S NOTE:

You'll notice that the recipe does not contain 20 garlic cloves, despite Ezra's recommendation. But he is cooking enough to serve an entire restaurant.

Serves 4

450g chicken gizzards
1 teaspoon salt
½ teaspoon pepper
2 tablespoons butter
3 garlic cloves, finely chopped
2 tablespoons flour

Put the chicken gizzards, salt and pepper in a large pan and add enough cold water to cover. Place over a medium heat and bring to the boil. Reduce the heat and simmer for 1 hour.

Remove the gizzards with a slotted spoon and chop coarsely. (You can also pulse these briefly in a food-processor.) Do not discard the broth. Melt the butter in a small frying pan over a medium heat and add the garlic and flour. Cook, stirring, for a minute or two to form a paste.

Bring the gizzard broth to the boil, stir a little of the broth into the garlic paste, then stir the paste back into the broth. Add the chopped gizzards and simmer for 15 minutes.

Season well with salt and pepper, and serve.

Alan De Fretais's
Aphrodisiac Asparagus

from *The Bedroom Secrets of the Master Chefs* by Irvine Welsh

The celebrated cook Alan De Fretais had recently courted controversy by publishing a book entitled *The Bedroom Secrets of the Master Chefs*. On the pages of this aphrodisiac cookbook, several internationally renowned culinary experts had each produced a recipe, writing about how they managed to use it to advance a seduction or to complement a lovemaking session. It quickly became a publishing sensation, spending several weeks heading the bestsellers list.

A middle-aged woman in fake fur appeared and threw her hands ceilingwards. — Alan! Darling, that book of yours is amazing. Tried the asparagus recipe on old Conrad and it was better than Viagra! I was planning to thank you from the bottom of my heart, but I'm thinking a little further down might be more appropriate.

— Delighted to be of service, Eilidh, De Fretais smiled, kissing the woman on both cheeks.

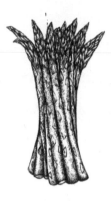

RECIPE:

Serves 2

FOR THE SAUCE

1 tbsp olive oil, plus extra to drizzle

½ red onion, finely chopped

½ head of fennel, finely chopped

½ red pepper, finely chopped

1 small red chilli, finely chopped

1 small garlic clove, crushed

200g chopped tomatoes

1 bay leaf

2 tbsp mascarpone

FOR THE ASPARAGUS AND NEW POTATOES
200g new potatoes, halved
12 asparagus spears
6 slices Parma ham

Heat the oil in a pan and stir in the onion, fennel and red pepper. Cook over a low heat for 5-8 minutes until the vegetables have started to soften and the onions start to turn golden.

Stir in the chilli and garlic and cook for 1 minute. Season well. Pour in the tomatoes and add the bay leaf to the pan with 100ml hot water. Cover the pan, bring to the boil and simmer for 15 minutes until thickened.

Preheat the oven to 200°C/180°C fan oven/gas mark 6. Line a roasting tin with baking parchment. Scatter over the new potatoes and drizzle with a little oil. Season well and roast in the oven for 10-15 minutes.

Wrap the asparagus spears in half a slice of Parma ham each. Brush with olive oil and add to the roasting tin with the potatoes. Continue to roast for a further 10 minutes.

Whizz the sauce until smooth, then stir in the mascarpone and season well.

Divide the potatoes and asparagus between two plates, spoon the sauce into two small pots and serve together, scattered with basil.

MAIN COURSES

The Dowager's Salade Niçoise

from *1Q84* (Book 1) by Haruki Murakami

Tamaru rolled their meal in on a wagon. A professional chef had doubtless prepared the food, but it was Tamaru's job to serve it. He plucked the bottle of white wine from its ice bucket and poured with practiced movements. The dowager and Aomame both tasted the wine. It had a lovely bouquet and was perfectly chilled. The dinner consisted of boiled white asparagus, *salade niçoise*, a crabmeat omelet, and rolls and butter, nothing more. All the ingredients were fresh and delicious, and the portions were moderate. The dowager always ate small amounts of food. She used her knife and fork elegantly, bringing one tiny bite after another to her mouth like a small bird. Tamaru stayed in the farthest corner of the room throughout the meal. Aomame was always amazed how such a powerfully built man could obscure his own presence for such a long time.

The two women spoke only in brief snatches during the meal, concentrating instead on what they ate. Music played at low volume – a Haydn cello concerto. This was another of the dowager's favorites.

After the dishes were taken away, a coffeepot arrived. Tamaru poured, and as he backed away, the dowager turned to him with a finger raised.

'Thank you, Tamaru. That will be all.'

Tamaru nodded respectfully and left the room, his footsteps silent as always. The door closed quietly behind him. While the two women drank their coffee, the music ended and a new silence came to the room.

'You and I trust each other, wouldn't you say?' the dowager said, looking straight at Aomame.

Aomame agreed – succinctly, but without reservation.

'We share some important secrets,' the dowager said. 'We have put our fates in each other's hands.'

Aomame nodded silently.

This was the room in which Aomame first confessed her secret to the dowager.

RECIPE:
Serves 4

FOR THE DRESSING
½ garlic clove, crushed
3 tablespoons extra-virgin olive oil
1 tablespoon white wine vinegar
1 teaspoon Dijon mustard
Squeeze of lemon

FOR THE SALAD
4 tuna steaks, approximately 175g each,
no thicker than 1 inch
400g new potatoes, halved
150g green beans, trimmed
4 eggs
2 ripe tomatoes
½ small head of lettuce, leaves separated and washed
2 tablespoons black olives, pitted
½ red onion, finely sliced
8 basil leaves, roughly torn
8 anchovies, preserved in oil

Whisk together all the ingredients for the dressing, along with a teaspoon of cold water. Place the tuna steaks in a glass bowl, pour a quarter of the dressing over them, cover with clingfilm and leave in the fridge for 1–2 hours to marinate.

Bring a pan of salted water to the boil, add the new potatoes and cook for 12–15 minutes until tender. Add the green beans to the pan for the last 3–4 minutes of cooking. Drain well.

Meanwhile, bring a separate pan of water to the boil and cook the eggs for 7 minutes. Transfer to a bowl of cold water and allow to cool. When cool enough to handle, peel off the shells.

Cut a cross in the top of the tomatoes then put into a bowl. Pour over enough boiling water to cover them and leave for a couple of minutes. Drain well and peel away and discard the skin; it should slip off easily. Cut each tomato into quarters, then tease out the seeds with a teaspoon and discard.

When your tuna steaks have marinated, heat a griddle over a high heat. Once the pan is hot, cook the steaks for 2–3 minutes on each side, depending on how well cooked you like your tuna steak.

Arrange the washed and dried lettuce leaves on a large plate or in a large bowl. Scatter over the potatoes, followed by the green beans and the tomatoes. Cut the eggs into quarters and arrange on the top followed by the black olives, red onion and basil. Slice the tuna steaks diagonally and place them on top, followed by the anchovies. Spoon the remaining dressing over the salad and serve.

The Novelist's Lamb Stew

from the short story 'Homage to Hemingway'
by Julian Barnes

On the last evening, he cooked a gigantic stew and provided so many bottles of wine that they didn't need the pub. Responding to their praise, he told them his theory of writers and cooking. Novelists, who were in it for the long haul, were temperamentally equipped for stewing and braising, for the slow mixing together of many ingredients; whereas poets ought to be good at stir-fry. And short-story writers? someone asked. Steak and chips. Dramatists? Ah, dramatists – they, the lucky sods, were basically mere orchestrators of the talents of others, so would be satisfied with shaking a leisurely cocktail while the kitchen staff rustled up the grub. This went down well, and they started fantasising about the sort of food famous writers would serve. Jane Austen and Bath buns. The Brontës and Yorkshire pudding. There was even an argument when Virginia Woolf and cucumber sandwiches were put together. But without any discord they placed Hemingway in front of an enormous barbecue piled with marlin steaks and cuts of buffalo, a beer in one hand and an outsized spatula in the other, while the party swirled around him.

RECIPE:

Serves 4

2 tablespoons oil
1 large onion, chopped
2 carrots, chopped
2 celery sticks, chopped
500g boneless lamb leg, fat trimmed and
cut into 5cm cubes
1 tablespoon plain flour
900ml fresh lamb or chicken stock
100ml red wine
1 rosemary sprig, leaves chopped
1 teaspoon tomato purée
2–3 dashes of Worcestershire sauce
6 small potatoes, peeled and quartered
Salt and freshly ground black pepper

Heat half the oil in a large casserole pan. Add the onion, carrot and celery, season well with salt and pepper and sauté over a medium heat for about 10 minutes. Cook until the edges of the vegetables have caramelised slightly and turned golden. Spoon onto a plate and set aside.

Add the remaining oil to the pan and brown the lamb in batches of three or four pieces at a time. Season the meat once cooked, then spoon onto the plate with the vegetables.

Preheat the oven to 170°C/150°C fan oven/gas mark 3.

When all the pieces of lamb have been browned, stir the flour into the oil in the base of the pan and cook for 1 minute. Slowly stir in the stock and red wine and add the rosemary, tomato purée and Worcestershire sauce. Return the meat and vegetables to the pan.

Cover the pan with a lid and bring the stew to a simmer, about 5 minutes. Once it's simmering, transfer the casserole to the oven and cook for 1 hour.

Add the potatoes to the pan and stir everything together, then return to the oven for a further 30 minutes, until the potatoes are tender. Taste and adjust the seasoning and serve.

Cephallonian Meat Pie
(suitable for vegetarians)

from *Captain Corelli's Mandolin* by Louis de Bernières

Carlo and the captain uneasily partook of the tiny spinach pies, the fried baby squid and the dolmades stuffed with rice. The doctor glowered at them, inwardly delighted with the successful inauguration of his novel project for resistance, and the two soldiers avoided his gaze, commenting politely and inconsequentially upon the beauty of the night, the impossible size of the olive tree, and any and every irrelevance that occurred to them.

Carlo drove gratefully away, and the captain sat on Pelagia's bed miserably. It was the time for an evening meal, and despite the plates of appetisers his stomach growled from force of habit. The thought of more of that wonderful food left him feeling weak.

Father and daughter sat down to eat, both of them clattering the cutlery on the plates, and waited until they were sure that the Italian must be dying of hunger and feeling like a ragamuffin boy who has been sent to Coventry at school, and then they invited him to join them. He sat with them and ate in silence.

'This is Cephallonian meat pie,' said the doctor in an informative tone of voice, 'except that, thanks to your people, it doesn't have any meat in it.'

Afterwards, when the curfew patrol had already passed, the doctor announced his intention to go for a walk. 'But the curfew ...' protested Corelli, and the doctor replied, 'I was born here, this is my island.' He gathered up his hat and his pipe, and swept out.

RECIPE:

Serves 6–8

1 tablespoon olive oil

Knob of butter

1 small red onion, finely chopped

1 celery stick, finely sliced

40g green beans, sliced

65g Arborio rice

150ml vegetable stock

7 sheets of filo pastry

1 large egg

50g feta cheese, crumbled

Handful toasted pine nuts

Zest of ¼ lemon

1 tablespoon each freshly chopped parsley, mint and thyme

1–2 tablespoons sesame seeds

Salt and freshly ground black pepper

Heat the oil and half the butter in a pan with 2 tablespoons of water. Once the butter has melted, add the red onion and celery and cook gently until the onion has softened – this usually takes 10–15 minutes.

Stir in the green beans and cook for a further minute, then add the rice and stir to make sure it's well mixed into the vegetables. Season well with salt and pepper. Pour in the stock, cover with a lid and bring to the boil. Turn the heat down low and simmer for 5 minutes until the stock has been absorbed. Spoon the rice mixture into a bowl and allow to cool.

Preheat the oven to 200°C/fan oven 180°C/gas mark 6 and put a baking sheet in the oven.

Melt the remaining butter in a small pan. Spread one sheet of the filo pastry with melted butter and use it to line a shallow 20cm cake tin so it comes up and over the sides by about half a centimetre. Repeat this process with another 4 sheets of filo pastry.

Beat the egg in a bowl and reserve about a tablespoon of beaten egg to glaze the pastry. Add the remaining egg to the rice mixture with the feta, pine nuts, lemon zest and herbs and fold well to combine. Season with salt and pepper.

Spoon into the pastry-lined tin and spread over the base evenly. Fold the edge of the pastry sheets over the rice mixture, using the additional two sheets to cover the top if needed. Brush the remaining egg all over the top of the pastry. Sprinkle with the sesame seeds and bake in the oven for 25–30 minutes, until the pastry is golden and crisp and the pie is cooked through.

Henry Perowne's Seafood Stew

from *Saturday* by Ian McEwan

With the idea of the news, inseparable from it, at least at weekends, is the lustrous prospect of a glass of red wine. He empties the last of a Côtes du Rhône into a glass, puts the TV on mute and sets about stripping and chopping three onions. Impatient of the papery outer layers, he makes a deep incision, forcing his thumb in four layers deep and ripping them away, wasting a third of the flesh. He chops the remainder rapidly and tips it into a casserole with a lot of olive oil. What he likes about cooking is its relative imprecision and lack of discipline – a release from the demands of the operating theatre. In the kitchen, the consequences of failure are mild: disappointment, a wisp of disgrace, rarely voiced. No one actually dies. He strips and chops eight fat cloves of garlic and adds them to the onions. From recipes he draws only the broadest principles. The cookery writers he admires speak of 'handfuls' and 'a sprinkling', of 'chucking in' this or that. They list alternative ingredients and encourage experimentation. Henry accepts that he'll never make a decent cook, that he belongs to what

Rosalind calls the hearty school. Into his palm he empties several dried red chillies from a pot and crushes them between his hands and lets the flakes fall with their seeds into the onions and garlic. The TV news comes up but he doesn't touch the mute. It's the same helicopter shot from before it got dark, the same crowds still filing into the park, the same general celebration. Onto the softened onions and garlic – pinches of saffron, some bay leaves, orange-peel gratings, oregano, five anchovy fillets, two tins of peeled tomatoes. ... From the fridge he takes a quarterfull bottle of white wine, a Sancerre, and tips it over the tomato mix.

On a broader, thicker chopping block, Perowne arranges the monkfish tails and cuts them into chunks and tips them into a big white bowl. Then he washes the ice off the tiger prawns and puts them in too. In a second bowl, he puts the clams and mussels. Both bowls go into the fridge, with dinner plates as lids.

His preparations are done, just as the burning plane story comes up, fourth item. With a confused sense that he's about to learn something significant about himself, he turns on the sound and stands facing the tiny set, drying his hands on a towel.

RECIPE:

Serves 10

6 tablespoons good-flavoured olive oil, plus extra to serve

3 onions, chopped

8 garlic cloves, chopped

3–4 dried chillies, crumbled

Pinch of saffron threads

1–2 bay leaves

Zest of ¼ orange

1 teaspoon dried oregano or 1 tablespoon freshly chopped
oregano

5 anchovy fillets, preserved in oil

2 x 400g tins peeled plum tomatoes

3 skate wing skeletons

500g mussels, well scrubbed and debearded

175ml dry white wine, Sancerre for preference

2 x 500g monkfish tails, skinned and removed from the bone

300g raw tiger prawns

500g clams, well scrubbed

Salt and freshly ground black pepper

Lemon wedges, to serve

Pour 2 litres water into a large pan and bring to the boil.

Put the olive oil and chopped onions into another large pan and place over a medium heat. Stir every now and then to ensure the onions aren't browning too much. After about 10 minutes, stir in the garlic then crumble in the dried chillies. Add the saffron, bay leaves, orange zest and oregano and stir everything together. Season well with salt and pepper. Drop the anchovy fillets into the pan along with the plum tomatoes, using a wooden spoon to break the tomatoes up into the sauce.

Drop the skate wings into the boiling water and reduce the heat to a simmer. Add a handful of the mussels and cover the pan with a lid. Simmer for 15 minutes to create a flavoursome stock.

Pour the white wine into the tomato sauce and return to a simmer, stirring regularly. Strain the fish stock into the pan of simmering tomato sauce, discarding the skate wings and boiled mussels, and cook for a further 5 minutes.

Chop the monkfish roughly into 5cm pieces. Add to the pan, along with the remaining mussels, the prawns and the clams and tuck under the sauce. Simmer gently for 10 minutes or until all the fish is opaque. Taste and adjust the seasoning. Spoon into bowls and serve with lemon wedges and a drizzle of oil over the top.

Risotto Londis

from *The Red House* by Mark Haddon

Angela poured boiling water over the dried mushrooms. A smell like unwashed bodies she always thought, but it was the simplest vegetarian recipe she knew. Made her want to roast a pig's head for Melissa, all glossy crackling and an apple in the mouth. Make Benjy sad, though. Earlier she had told Dominic that she wanted to go home, and thought for a moment that he might actually agree but he had slipped into the grating paternal role he'd been adopting more and more over the last few days. *You'll regret it…insult to Richard …hang on in there…* Him being right made it worse, of course. Sherry, tomato purée. Risotto Londis.

Louisa came into the kitchen, placed a glass of red wine in front of her and retreated to the window seat. Some change in her aura that Angela couldn't pinpoint. *Sorry about last night.*

Last night? Angela had suppressed the memory so well that it took a few seconds to unearth. *I think it's me who should apologise.*

RECIPE:

Serves 4

25g dried porcini mushrooms
2 tablespoons olive oil
2 knobs of butter
1 onion, finely chopped
1 garlic clove, crushed
250g chestnut mushrooms, sliced
300g risotto rice
100ml dry white wine
900ml hot vegetable stock
1–2 tablespoons freshly grated Parmesan,
plus extra to serve
2 tablespoons sunflower oil
10–12 fresh sage leaves
Salt and freshly ground black pepper

Put the dried mushrooms in a bowl and pour over 200ml boiling water. Leave to soak for 10–15 minutes to extract the flavour.

Line a sieve with a clean j-cloth and strain the mushroom liquor into a saucepan over the lowest heat to keep warm. Finely chop the soaked mushrooms, squeezing them gently to remove excess liquid.

Heat the oil and a knob of butter in a pan and sauté the onion over a low heat for around 15 minutes, until softened but not coloured. Stir in the garlic and dried and fresh mushrooms then cook for 1 minute. Stir in the rice and cook for a few minutes so that the grains are heated through and coated in the oil. Pour in the wine – you should hear a big sigh – and stir in.

Allow the rice to absorb most of the liquid, then pour in the reserved mushroom liquor. Continue to stir, ensuring the rice absorbs most of the liquid. As soon as it does, add a ladleful of hot stock and continue to stir.

Add all the stock in this way and cook until it's almost all absorbed. Stir in a knob of butter and a little Parmesan, then taste and adjust the seasoning.

When the risotto is almost ready and has a creamy texture, heat the sunflower oil in a separate pan. When it is hot, add the sage leaves and lightly sauté until they are crisp – this should only take a few seconds. Remove them onto a paper towel to absorb the excess oil.

Spoon the risotto into bowls, grating over more Parmesan as desired, and top with the crispy sage leaves.

Day Three: Rice, Kichadi Beans and Curried Tofu

from *Sex is Forbidden* by Tim Parks

I love washing rice and kichada beans. The rice is milky white, the beans bright yellow. 'Mix together rice and beans in equal amounts in eight oven trays and rinse clean.' I use lukewarm water. The steel trays fit neatly over the sink under the tap. Three rinses, the recipe says. I never do less than four. If you use cold water your fingers freeze and you can't enjoy it. In the warm water the grains feel delicate and friendly, you can imagine you're moving your fingers in someone's hair. Stupid. The thing is not to imagine anything, just to be happy with white rice and yellow kichada beans. As soon as you run the water in the tray everything goes milky. The rice disappears and the tiny beans lose their yellowness. The water turns soft and slippery on your fingers as you run them back and forth through a sludge of grains. Tip the pan gently to drain and the white and yellow come back, but changed, softened.

At the second rinse, the cloudiness is thinner, like muslin curtains, or mist when you're in a plane and the ground shows pale beneath. When we went to Berlin. No. Like itself, like nothing but itself. Water rinsing rice. The third time you have to work hard to bring out a few wisps of milkiness. Probably the recipe's right and a fourth rinse is unnecessary, but I like to watch the clear water run over the clean wet grains. There is something specially lovely about seeing things through clean water, even if they're not lovely in themselves. Carrots, celery, even turnips. Like when you've meditated for two hours straight, all the thoughts and mental mess have settled, your head is clear, and when you put on your shoes again and step out of the Metta Hall every blade of grass, the leaves on the trees, even people's clothes on the washing line have a transparent underwater weirdness.

RECIPE:
Serves 4

FOR THE RICE AND LENTILS
200g basmati rice, soaked for 30 minutes
75g split pigeon pea lentils (*toovar* or *toor dal*),
soaked for 3–4 hours
Small knob of ghee or butter

FOR THE TOFU CURRY
2 tablespoons vegetable oil, plus a little extra
1 onion, finely chopped
1 garlic clove, crushed
2cm piece of fresh ginger, peeled and grated
½ teaspoon chilli powder
1 teaspoon each ground coriander and cumin
1 green chilli, finely chopped
1 teaspoon garam masala
½ teaspoon turmeric
400g tin tomatoes
400g firm tofu, drained and cut into 2.5cm cubes

100g frozen peas, defrosted

Large handful of spinach, chopped

Salt and freshly ground black pepper

1 tablespoon freshly chopped coriander, to garnish

Rinse the rice and lentils in three or four changes of cold water until the water runs clear. Put in a pan with 750ml water and bring to the boil. Turn the heat down to the lowest setting, put a lid on the pan to keep in the steam, and cook for 30–40 minutes until all the liquid has absorbed and the lentils are tender.

Meanwhile make the tofu curry. Heat the oil in a pan and fry the onion, garlic and ginger over a medium heat until the onion starts to turn golden. Stir in the chilli powder, ground coriander and cumin, green chilli, garam masala and turmeric. Cook for 1–2 minutes, then add a tablespoon of water at a time until the oil starts to separate from the mixture. Stir in the tomatoes and 200ml water and season well. Bring to the boil, then reduce the heat to low and simmer for 20 minutes, leaving the pan uncovered to reduce the curry.

Heat a little oil in a frying pan and stir-fry the tofu pieces, in batches, until golden on all sides, adding more oil as necessary. Drain on kitchen paper.

Stir the peas and spinach into the spiced tomato base and then add the fried tofu. Taste and adjust the seasoning. Add the ghee or butter to the drained rice and lentils and use a fork to fluff up the rice. Serve both together and garnish with the fresh coriander.

Jeanette's Hand-caught Rabbit Stew

On the occasion of finding a rabbit in her vegetable garden, Jeanette Winterson took to Twitter to update her followers on how the rabbit fared:

18.10 | Rabbit ate my parsley. I am eating the rabbit.

18.14 | FYI! My rabbit traps are cages. Rabbit in, you dispatch it humanely OF COURSE! Rabbits look cute but the eco-balance is out this year

18.46 | Here is the rabbit washed and jointed for the pot

18.58 | On the AGA in cider with rosemary and thyme

19.10 | Here is my cat eating the rabbit innards. No waste no packaging no processing no food miles.

19.52 | RABBITS! Fascinated by the vast conversation. I eat wild game & fish. Learned to skin, pluck, gut, bone

19.59 | For all the Tweeters who said my cat would prefer Whiskers – where do u think pet food comes from BTW?

RECIPE:

Serves 2

1 whole rabbit (wild for preference)
250ml French cider, plus extra to wash it down with
5 or 6 shallots
Pinch of salt
Sprig of fresh rosemary
1 bulb fennel, finely sliced
2 tbsp double cream
Oil, for frying
New potatoes or bread, to serve

FOR THOSE STARTING FROM SCRATCH:

First, catch your rabbit. If you can shoot your own, then wild rabbits are best – rearing conditions for farmed rabbits are far from ideal, and wild rabbit is one of the most humane and nutritious things you can eat.

If your rabbit is in his jacket, you will need to slip it off. Cut off the feet, then slit the skin up the stomach and slide your hand inside to the flank, working round to the saddle, and pull the rabbit out neatly in one piece. Then cut off the head. You should now have a rabbit-skin glove puppet.

Pouch your rabbit with one quick cut (remove innards) and feed the contents to your cat or dog.

Swill out the cavity with water.

Joint the rabbit neatly – legs, saddle and shoulders. Arrange the meat on a plate (out of dog or cat's reach), lightly salt to soak up the excess moisture, and pat dry.

FOR THOSE OPTING FOR A PRE-BUTCHERED RABBIT, START HERE:

If your rabbit came from the butcher or farmers' market, it will already be pouched and jointed.

Brown the cut-up rabbit in oil for about 5 minutes; the oil should be hot enough to sizzle when the meat is put in the pan.

Add the cider, and reduce down – this should take around half an hour.

Meanwhile, in a separate pan sauté the shallots in olive oil until soft along with the salt, rosemary and slices of fennel.

Add this mixture to the rabbit and simmer for around 20 minutes.

Just before serving, remove the stew from the heat and stir in a little bit of cream.

Serve with new potatoes or bread (or whatever takes your fancy), and wash down with some French cider.

(Cook's note: you may not want to broadcast your meal on Twitter.)

DESSERTS

Apricot Ischl Tarts

from *Human Traces* by Sebastian Faulks

Valade invited himself to stay at the schloss, insisting that it be as a patient. 'Melancholy' was his self-diagnosis, though there was little sign of it in his behaviour, and he resisted Thomas's offer of a consultation.

'Perhaps you should see my colleague, Dr Rebière, if you would find it awkward to speak to me.'

'I have no desire to talk about my private thoughts to a man I barely know,' said Valade. 'To tell a stranger my inner feelings! It is a barbaric idea. I ask only to be allowed the peace and quiet of the sanatorium and to feed myself on its excellent cooking.'

At dinner that night, he placed himself at the only spare place, which was at a table with two neurasthenic young women, Fräulein Fuchs and Fräulein Wolf, and an elderly German lawyer, Herr Hassler, who suffered bouts of mania in which he believed himself to be the king of Prussia.

'Boy!' called Valade to the startled Hans, who was helping as a waiter. 'Bring me a bottle of the best red burgundy in the house. Ladies, will you do me the honour of taking wine with me?'

Valade asked Hans to deliver champagne to all the tables in the dining room, to go with the black cherry cake and apricot Ischl tarts that the girls were bringing in from the kitchen. After dinner, he persuaded Fräulein Wolf to play the piano in the hall, while he commanded Hans to bring more champagne for those who stayed to listen. The party went on till midnight, when Sonia was persuaded to play 'The Lincolnshire Poacher' and Jacques sang a song in French: 'There was a little ship…'

RECIPE:

Makes about 18 biscuits

60g softened butter
15g cream cheese
75g golden caster sugar
1 tablespoon beaten egg
110g plain flour, plus extra for rolling
1/8 teaspoon baking powder
15g ground almonds
½ teaspoon grated lemon zest
Apricot jam, for filling
Icing sugar, to dust

Put the butter, cream cheese and sugar in a large bowl and beat until soft and creamy. Add the egg and beat until smooth.

Sift over the flour and baking powder and start to work it into the mixture. When half is worked in, add the ground almonds and lemon zest and continue to gradually mix the dry ingredients into the butter mixture. Bring together with your hands and knead to make a smooth dough. Wrap in baking parchment and chill for 1 hour.

Preheat the oven to 180°C/fan oven 160°C/gas mark 4. Line two baking sheets with baking paper.

Divide the dough in half. Generously dust your work surface with flour and roll out one half of the dough to a thickness of about 2mm. Use a 5cm cutter to cut out 18 rounds. Transfer to a prepared baking sheet.

Repeat with the remaining dough, rerolling as necessary, but this time cutting out a small circle from the middle of each round using the bottom of a piping nozzle – this is so that you can see the jam when you sandwich the two halves together. Bake in the oven for 8–10 minutes until just golden. Immediately transfer to a wire rack to cool.

Spoon a little jam onto the biscuit rounds, then put the biscuits with a hole in the middle on top. Dust with icing sugar and serve.

Cinnamon and Honey Ice Cream

from *Scribble, Scribble, Scribble* by Simon Schama

The delirium of ice cream is inseparable from juvenile glee; the uninhibited indulgence of the mouth. To get your tongue round a dollop is to become instantaneously childlike again, whatever your age; to cop a mouthful of lusciousness that magically marries opposites: fruit and dairy, the tart and the voluptuous; a shot of excitement meets a scoop of all's well. Yes, yes, doctor, we know the taking of the coneheaped mound in our greedy gobs makes us blissed-out babies again, tripping down mammary lane: slurp, lick, suck, even, on occasions, drool and slobber. But it's more complicated than milky regression.

The past masters of ice-cream making knew all about the lure of the savoury. Frederick Nutt's *Complete Confectioner of 1789* offered thirty-two flavours, including barberry, brown bread, damson and Parmesan cheese, which turns out to be nothing more than a frozen soufflé and lacks the conviction of his 'grape' flavour (actually made with elder, the *grappe de sureau*). If it's serious shock-ice you're hunting, you need to hop on a plane to Otaru Unga in Hokkaido, Japan, where apparently you can sample their chicken-wing, horse-flesh, sea-urchin, squid-ink, crab and (less dauntingly) pickled-plum and cherry-blossom flavours. Beside those exercises in kamikaze infusions, our home-grown Purbeck's Chilli Red seems hopelessly sedate, its speckling of hot flakes neutralised by the ocean of fatty Dorset cream.

Gael Greene, the food critic of *New York Magazine*, claimed that it was 'not excessive to rank the ice-cream revolution with the sexual revolution, the women's movement and peace for our time'. 'Great ice cream,' she wrote, as if declaiming the Gettysburg Address, 'is sacred, brave, an eternal verity.' Jeez, Gael, it ain't that good, but okay, it's pretty damned close.

RECIPE:

COOK'S NOTE:

Cinnamon loses its strength very easily, and for this recipe to work the spice needs to infuse the custard. So if, when you open the jar or bruise the end of a stick, you don't get a fierce shot of fragrance, buy some fresh cinnamon.

serves 6–10

1½ cinnamon sticks, broken in half
250ml full-fat milk
650ml cream
2 tablespoons ground cinnamon
3 tablespoons clear honey
6 egg yolks
50g caster sugar
Brandy snaps, to serve

Put the cinnamon sticks in a small frying pan over a medium-low heat and dry roast until they release their fragrance. Be careful not to burn the sticks. Then put the milk, half the cream and the sticks into a medium, heavy-based pan and whisk in the ground cinnamon. Bring almost (but not completely) to the boil, stirring continuously. Reduce the heat, add the honey and stir for a further 5 minutes so that the cinnamon can infuse. Remove from the heat and leave to stand for 5 minutes, then remove the cinnamon sticks.

In a large bowl, whisk the egg yolks with the sugar until the mixture is pale yellow. Pour 50ml of the hot milk mixture into the egg and sugar and whisk until well combined; then gradually whisk in the rest. Return to the pan and stir over a low heat for 7–10 minutes until the custard coats the back of a spoon. Remove from the heat and leave to cool completely.

Taste for fragrance. If it's a little underwhelming, this is the moment you can, if you like, add some super-high-quality ground cinnamon. It will fleck the ice cream, but what's wrong with that?

Whip the remainder of the cream to soft peaks and fold into the mixture. Chill for at least 5 hours in the fridge or, better still, overnight. Turn the mixture into an ice-cream maker and churn following the manufacturer's instructions.

Serve with brandy snaps.

Fernandez's Classic English Trifle in India

from *The Best Exotic Marigold Hotel* by Deborah Moggach

Evelyn was thinking about her own son. She was looking forward to his visit with mixed feelings. Of course she wanted to see him, and the grandchildren whom she had not seen for so long, but she simply couldn't imagine Christopher in India. How would he react to this place? … What would he think of the palsied servants, of the taps that coughed out brown water? Maybe he would sweep up Evelyn and take her back to New York. If he were Indian he would do that, but then if he were Indian he would never have let his mother come here in the first place.

Actually, thought Evelyn, I wouldn't want to go. Sitting there at dinner, she realised she had grown fond of her fellow residents. They were all in the same boat, all deserted in one way or another by those they had loved, and now they had to stick together. After two months they had become a sort of family; even those she didn't particularly like had grown so familiar that concepts of liking or disliking had become irrelevant. England was distant now, it was another life; it was these people now who concerned her. Some might get ill and go into hospital. Some might succumb to homesickness and return to Britain. The slightly odd ones would no doubt become odder, herself included. Some might – they would – die. They would all die.

'You on for *Inspector Morse?*' asked Douglas.

Evelyn nodded. Graham's great-nephew had sent a video of *Inspector Morse* from England. Graham didn't look like the sort of man who had relatives, but he obviously had. Maybe nobody had asked him. Those not exhausted by the trip were planning to watch that nice John Thaw after dinner. Evelyn ate a mouthful of trifle. It was startlingly coloured, with hundreds and thousands on top. It reminded her of her children's birthday parties and there was a comfort in that. Whatever happened, there was always comfort to be found in the small things of life.

RECIPE:
Serves 6–8

FOR THE BASE
6–8 trifle sponges
2–3 tablespoons sherry
175g raspberries
1 packet raspberry jelly

FOR THE CUSTARD
3 medium egg yolks
3 tablespoons golden caster sugar
30g cornflour
1½ teaspoons vanilla extract
450ml full-fat milk

FOR THE CREAM AND TOPPING
150ml double cream
1 tablespoon golden caster sugar
Hundreds and thousands

Arrange the trifle sponges in the base of a large bowl so they sit in an even layer. Spoon over the sherry, then scatter the raspberries over the top. Break up the raspberry jelly and put it in a jug. Add 275ml boiling water and stir until all the cubes of jelly have dissolved. Pour over the sponge and fruit. Cool, then chill in the fridge until set.

To make the custard, put the egg yolks, sugar, cornflour and vanilla extract in a bowl with 2 tablespoons of the milk. Whisk everything together until smooth. Pour the remaining milk into a pan and bring just to boiling point; take off the heat as soon as you see bubbles appearing round the edge of the pan.

Carefully pour the hot milk onto the egg mixture and whisk well with a large balloon whisk. Pour this mixture back into the pan and heat gently. Whisk until the custard has thickened and just holds its shape when you stir the whisk round the pan. Spoon into a bowl, cover with cling film to prevent a skin from forming, and allow to cool.

Carefully spread the cooled custard over the fruit and jelly layer and chill again. Whip the double cream and caster sugar together in a bowl until just thick enough to form soft peaks. Spoon all over the custard then sprinkle with hundreds and thousands and serve.

Payesh: Bengali rice pudding

from *The Lives of Others* by Neel Mukherjee

This afternoon, while he was doing his usual three-times-a-week English tuition, Mala-mashi had brought in, halfway through the tutorial, three bowls of chilled rice pudding, one each for the two boys and one for the new English tutor.

'It was Bumba's birthday on Wednesday,' she announced coyly while handing out the bowls.

She stretched to identical cups and bowls for tutor and both students now – previously Sona had been given stainless steel while Bumba and the tutor got china – but took away with the other hand: she exited the room with a comment that left no one in any doubt that she grudged the little good she had done this neighbour's boy. Couched, of course, as caring affection.

Today it was a different variation. Today the rice pudding was laced with: 'Just because you've now moved to a big school, it doesn't mean that you can't have some of the rice pudding I made for your not-very-clever friend's birthday.'

Sona, cocooned for the most part against this kind of poison, stayed silent and ran his spoon through the rice: it was a luxurious version with sultanas and cashews. He put a spoonful in his mouth. It was so delicious, coating every millimetre inside his mouth with its silky richness, that he closed his eyes. On his birthdays, his mother struggled to make him the obligatory rice pudding; she had to make do with broken rice, rather than the expensive gobinda-bhog, while raisins and nuts were beyond her imagining. He felt almost physically swayed by a wave of pity for his mother. His eyes prickled and the rice pudding, now bitter in his mouth, refused to move down his obstructed throat. In fierce defiance he thought that his mother's rice pudding was the best in the world; this one in his wretched hand could not even begin to compare with it.

RECIPE:

NOTE FROM THE AUTHOR:

What cake is to Western birthdays, *payesh* is to Bengali ones. It is not a million miles from English rice pudding although there is one significant difference: *payesh* is traditionally eaten cold. Having said that, I think it is equally good eaten warmed up. It requires no special tricks, no prestidigitating skills, only time, and patience, which will be richly rewarded. Just don't stray from the instructions. And don't even think about using anything other than full-fat milk. Also, it gets better and better over time and will last in the fridge for a good 4–5 days after you've cooked it.

A heat diffuser, if you have one, would be useful for cooking this dish.

Serves 6–8

2 litres full-fat milk
100g short-grain pudding rice
100g caster sugar
15–20 golden raisins/sultanas (optional)
3–4 bay leaves
3–4 green cardamom pods, pounded coarsely
Handful of cashew nuts, toasted (optional)

Pour the milk into a large, deep, heavy-bottomed stainless steel or non-stick pan and place over a high heat (if you have a heat diffuser, place this on the flame and put the pan on the heat diffuser), then keep stirring the milk until it comes to the boil. This will take time, about 20 minutes. Do not be distracted from stirring or the milk will boil over.

The milk will foam and look as if it's in spate. Keep stirring continuously, with the heat slightly reduced, for another 20 minutes. Now add the rice with one hand while continuing to stir with the other – this is crucial in order to prevent the rice from clumping. This may look like a tiny amount of rice compared with the vast amount of milk but, trust me, it will all come together in the end.

Keep stirring regularly and frequently, watching that the milk doesn't catch at the bottom of the pan, or boil over. After a while, the rice will slowly start becoming visible in the sea of milk. The milk will reduce in volume and start thickening. This will take about 20–30 minutes. Do not lose patience.

When the milk has thickened and reduced in volume by half but the whole mixture is still somewhat soupy, take the pan off the heat. Stir in the sugar, raisins or sultanas, and bay leaves and return the pan to the heat, now turned very low, and stir for another 5–7 minutes or so, making sure the pudding never comes to the boil.

Turn off the heat, add the ground cardamom and mix well. Sprinkle with the toasted cashews, if using, then cover and let sit for at least half an hour before eating. It will continue to become more and more set over time.

CONDIMENTS

Mary's Mango Pickle of Guilt

from *Midnight's Children* by Salman Rushdie

Reverend Mother sat at the head of the dining-table, doling out food (Amina took plates to Ahmed, who stayed in bed, moaning from time to time, 'Smashed, wife! Snapped – like an icicle!'); while, in the kitchens, Mary Pereira took the time to prepare, for the benefit of their visitors, some of the finest and most delicate mango pickles, lime chutneys and cucumber kasaundies in the world. And now, restored to the status of daughter in her own home, Amina began to feel the emotions of other people's food seeping into her - because Reverend Mother doled out the curries and meatballs of intransigence, dishes imbued with the personality of their creator; Amina ate the fish salans of stubbornness and the birianis of determination. And, although Mary's pickles had a partially counteractive effect – since she had stirred into them the guilt of her heart, and the fear of discovery, so that, good as they tasted, they had the power of making those who ate them subject to nameless uncertainties and dreams of accusing fingers – the diet provided by Reverend Mother filled

Amina with a kind of rage, and even produced slight signs of improvement in her defeated husband.

RECIPE:

Makes 4 x 375g jars

4 green mangoes, around 1.7kg in total
1 tablespoon salt
250ml distilled malt vinegar
500g granulated sugar
2 garlic cloves, sliced
5cm piece of fresh ginger, peeled and chopped
1 teaspoon cumin seeds
1 teaspoon cardamom seeds
1 teaspoon coriander seeds
1 teaspoon whole cloves
1 teaspoon black peppercorns
½ teaspoon turmeric
½ teaspoon cayenne pepper

Slice the flesh off each mango, cutting carefully around the flat stone. Peel each half and slice thinly. Cut away any remaining flesh from around the stones, and put all the sliced mango in a large glass bowl. Stir in the salt, cover and leave overnight.

The next day, drain the mango in a colander. Tip the flesh into a preserving pan and add the vinegar. Bring gently to the boil, then simmer for 10 minutes to soften the fruit. Stir every now and then to turn the top layer of fruit to the bottom.

Add all the remaining ingredients and stir everything together. Increase the heat and boil rapidly for about 5 minutes. Reduce the heat slightly so that the mixture is simmering and cook for 30 minutes, until the syrup has thickened and the mango is soft and translucent.

Spoon into hot sterilised jars and seal immediately. Store in a cool dry place.

James Bond's Vinaigrette

from *Solo* by William Boyd

Bond swiftly made his dressing then his filet mignon – *à point* – arrived with a bowl of salad. He had ordered filet mignon because he didn't want a steak that overlapped his plate. It was nicely chargrilled on the outside, pink but not blue on the inside. Bond dressed the salad, seasoned his steak and took his first mouthful of claret. As he ate and drank he allowed himself to enjoy the fantasy that life was good and the world was on its proper course – this being the purpose of eating and drinking well, surely? He ended his meal with half of an avocado into which he poured what remained of his dressing. He drank a calvados, smoked a cigarette and called for the check. His culinary hunger assuaged, a new one replaced it. He was hungry for Blessing, for her slim active body. Hungry for her to give him more precise instructions about what she wanted him to do to her.

RECIPE:

5 tablespoons red wine vinegar*
1 tablespoon extra-virgin olive oil
1 garlic clove, halved and crushed
½ teaspoon Dijon mustard
1 teaspoon granulated sugar
Freshly ground black pepper

Whisk together the vinegar, olive oil, garlic, mustard and sugar in a small bowl, adding a good grind of black pepper to season. Remove the garlic before using to dress your salad.

* The vinegar overload is essential.

Acknowledgements

The publishers gratefully acknowledge permission to reprint copyright material from the following Vintage authors (details given of first publication):

Helen Fielding, *Bridget Jones's Diary* (Picador, 1996)

Susan Hill, *The Various Haunts of Men* (Chatto & Windus, 2004)

Anne Tyler, *Dinner at the Homesick Restaurant* (Chatto & Windus, 1982)

Irvine Welsh, *The Bedroom Secrets of the Master Chefs* (Jonathan Cape, 2006)

Haruki Murakami, *1Q84* (Book 1) (Harvill Secker, 2011)

Julian Barnes, 'Homage to Hemingway' (published in *Through the Window: Seventeen Essays (and one short story)*, Vintage, 2012)

Louis de Bernières, *Captain Corelli's Mandolin* (Martin Secker & Warburg Limited, 1994)

Ian McEwan, *Saturday* (Jonathan Cape, 2005)

Mark Haddon, *The Red House* (Jonathan Cape, 2012)

Tim Parks, *Sex is Forbidden* (first published under the title *The Server*, Harvill Secker, 2012)

Jeanette Winterson (from her own Twitter feed, 2014)

Sebastian Faulks, *Human Traces* (Hutchinson, 2005)

Simon Schama, *Scribble, Scribble, Scribble* (The Bodley Head, 2010)

Deborah Moggach, *The Best Exotic Marigold Hotel* (first published under the title *These Foolish Things*, Chatto & Windus, 2004)

Neel Mukherjee, *The Lives of Others* (Chatto & Windus, 2014)

Salman Rushdie, *Midnight's Children* (Jonathan Cape, 1981)

William Boyd, *Solo* (Jonathan Cape, 2013)